USING THIS GUIDE

This book is designed to guide you around the main features of Big Pit as it is today. You will learn something of the history of the Welsh coalfields, how they were formed, how they were mined and what life was like in the mining communities.

The map at the back shows the main parts of the site and the location of all amenities.

Practical information about your visit, such as parking, refreshments and access arrangements can be found on page 63.

Since April 2001, entry to all National Museum Wales museums has been free, thanks to support from the Welsh Assembly Government.

Big Pit, 1970

CONTENTS

INTRODUCTION

WELCOME TO BIG PIT

At the end of the nineteenth century Wales was one of the most important coal producing countries in the world. In 1913, when over 60 million tons were being produced from over 600 collieries, one in ten Welsh people were employed in the coal industry and many more were dependent on it for a living.

By the end of the twentieth century only one deep mine remained in Wales. The coal industry, the most important industrial, social and political force in modern Wales, had all but vanished.

Over the past two centuries hundreds of collieries have been closed in Wales and normally all traces of them are lost. Big Pit is the exception: a colliery that once employed 1,300 people and produced over a quarter of a million tons of coal a year is now preserved for posterity as a world class museum.

Despite this, Big Pit is still very much a coal mine: the buildings are much the same as they were when the mine closed in 1980 and the winding wheels still turn, but it's now tourists rather than miners who descend the shaft. With a former miner as a guide, visitors can experience for themselves something of what it meant to work in one of the harshest of working places.

Big Pit is special, a place that tells the fascinating story of coal mining and the way the industry shaped modern Wales. It's a tale of victory and defeat, joy and disaster, riches and starvation during one of the most dramatic periods of Welsh and world history.

Enter the world of Welsh Coal…

Big Pit, 1975

> **The Devil made coal, made it black like himself and hid it in the deepest recesses of the earth so that he might drive man mad in the finding of it.**
>
> *Nineteenth-century coal miner*

Coal is the compressed remains of the plants that grew in this area about 300 million years ago. At that time Wales was close to the equator and the climate was hot and humid. Thick forests grew on swampy plains and river banks. On the forest floor, dead and rotting plants formed thick layers of peat.

Sometimes floods covered the forests, killing the plants and depositing sand and mud on top of the peat. When the water level fell, the forests grew back, until they were submerged again by flooding. This cycle of growth, flooding, burial and re-growth happened many times over millions of years, building up thousands of metres of mud, sand and peat. The weight of the overlying layers compressed the lowest layers to form rock. The peat layers were compacted to form coal.

COAL IN WALES

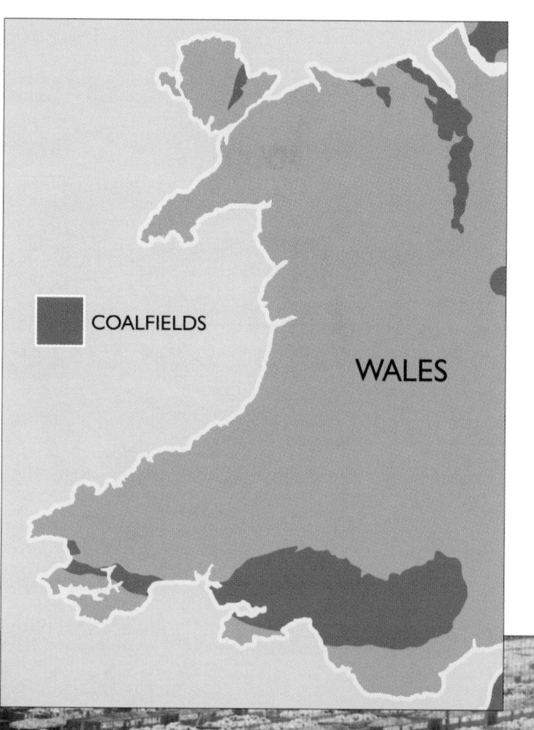

THE WELSH COALFIELDS

There are two major coalfields in Wales. The north Wales coalfield is forty-five miles long, nine miles at its widest point and is divided by the Bala fault. The northern portion, almost wholly in Flintshire, extends in a south easterly direction from Point of Ayr on the coast to Hawarden and Broughton near Chester. The Denbighshire portion is to the south. Heavily faulted and inclined seams make it difficult to mine this coal.

Coal wagons, Roath Dock, Cardiff, 1927

The fortunes of the north Wales coalfield tended to follow that of the local iron industry, the rapid growth of which led to a large influx of immigrant workers. Between 1870 and 1913 the annual output was between two and three million tons. However, industry gradually declined and by 1974 only two deep mines were in operation. Point of Ayr, the last colliery in north Wales, closed in 1996.

The south Wales coalfield extends from Pontypool in the east to St Brides Bay, Pembrokeshire, in the west. It is nearly ninety miles long and sixteen miles at its widest point. The total area covers some thousand square miles.

The coalfield forms an elongated basin dipping from the rim to the centre. The rim is where the coal seams were easiest to get at, so that's where mining activity started. The seams in the centre of the coalfield were the last to be exploited, as they were deeper and more difficult to mine.

The second half of the nineteenth century was a boom period for south Wales and, by 1913, the coalfield had reached its peak output of 57 million tons, with 232,800 men working in 620 mines. However, the district suffered a prolonged industrial depression from the early 1920s; by 1936, 241 collieries had closed and the workforce had halved to 130,000.

The coal industry remained important to south Wales and there were still 135 major collieries when the industry was nationalised in 1947. The slow decline continued however, and by 2004 there was just one deep mine in operation.

COAL IN WALES

THE USES OF COAL

North Wales coals are mostly high volatile, medium to strong coking coals used for metal manufacturing and the heating of homes.

South Wales has a larger variety of coal types. Anthracite is found to the west between the Gwendraeth valley and Hirwaun; steam coal is found in the central district between the Neath and Taff valleys; coking coal is found in Swansea to the south and gas bituminous coal in Blaenafon, to the north-east. These coals have a wide range of uses including domestic, steam raising, coke production for smelting metals and for the production of gas.

There are also a surprising number of everyday objects that use the by-products of coal in their manufacture, such as billiard balls, insecticides, storage batteries, perfumes, roofing and baking powders!

A NATION BUILT ON COAL

Well over three thousand million tons of coal have been mined in Wales – but there are over eight thousand million tons of coal still underground.

(Based on National Coal Board estimates, 1957)

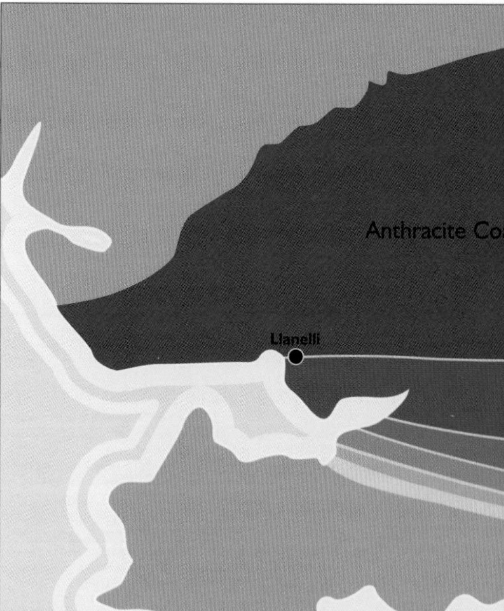

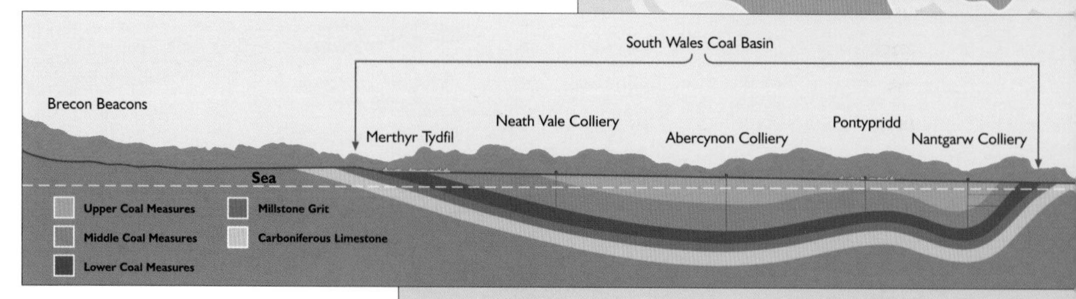

BLAENAFON COAL

Eleven different coal seams have been worked at Big Pit. The coal was reasonably good coking coal, but its steam-raising properties also put it into the category of steam coal, for which Wales was famous.

Blaenavon coal had great steam raising powering properties in conjunction with low ash and an unusually low percentage of sulphur – the latter prevents clinkering. Owing to its binding properties there is a complete absence of sparking, a quality of first importance with railways running through hot countries – also a large proportion goes for steamships.

South Wales Coal Annual 1907

The London and North Western Railway and Great Western Railways were both regular customers, as was the first railway of France – Chemin de Fer de L'Ouest. Regular shipments of Blaenafon coal were also made to South America and India.

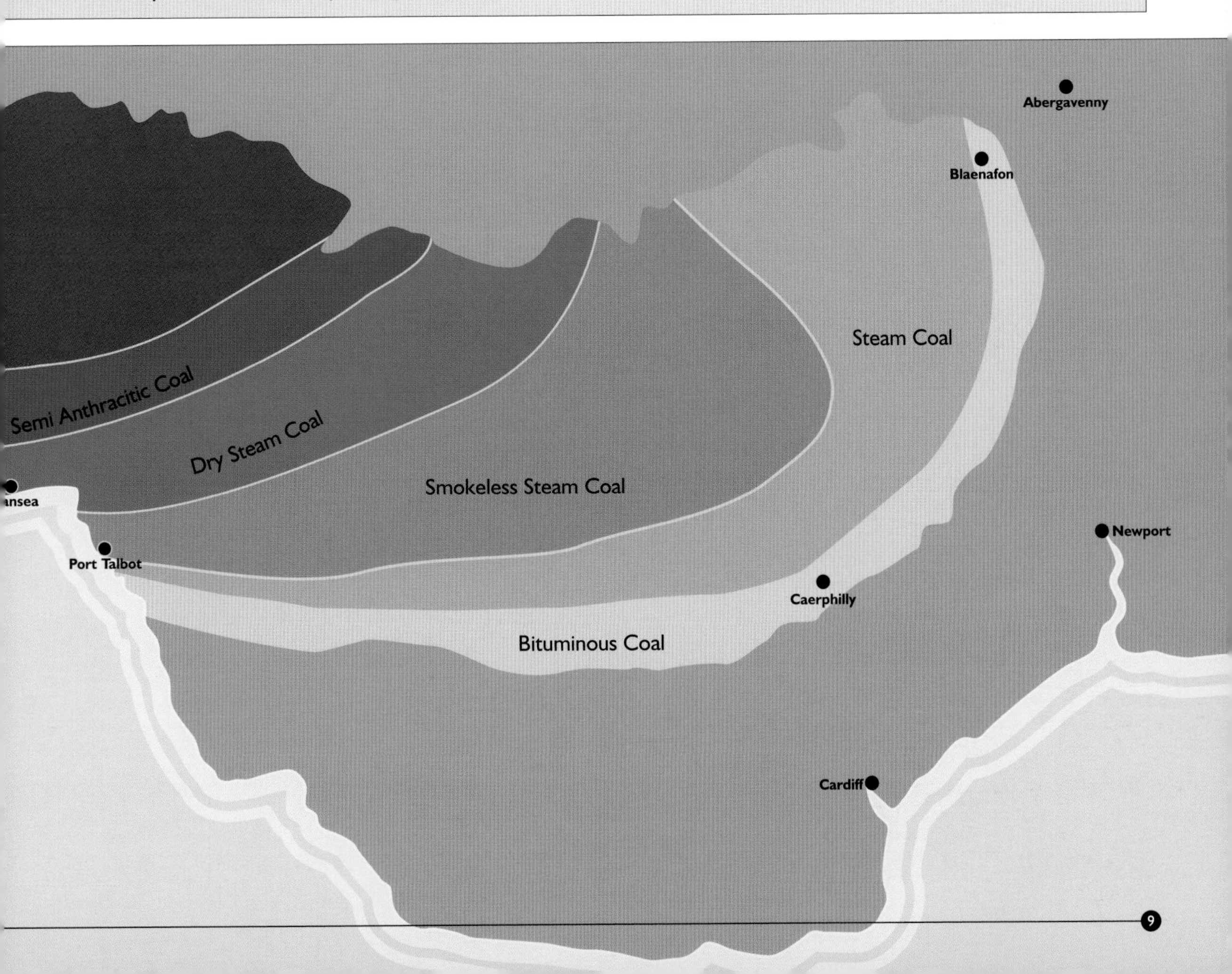

When I came to the pit they were working the last seam – we had a 2'4" section of coal to work using ploughs. The conditions were wet, damp and cold and of course the coal had got so thin that men were working literally lying flat on their bellies along the face. No longer could we use the approved supports that we were bound by law to use – and having come to that point then there was no way we could continue working.

Glyn Morgan, mine manager, Big Pit, 1973-1980

The new drift, 1976

MINING AT BIG PIT

Many mines in the Blaenafon area pre-date Big Pit. It is possible that ironstone and coal from the area may have been used by the Romans in their forts at Caerleon and Abergavenny, and there is clear evidence of medieval workings on the slopes of the Blorenge Mountain to the north-east of Blaenafon.

South Wales has large ironstone beds interspersed with the coal seams, and the geology of the coalfield causes both minerals to outcrop at the surface around the outer rim. The northern rim, which includes the Blaenafon area, had the further advantage of seams that were easier to mine. This, along with the local availability of limestone used in the metal smelting process, a high rainfall to provide water power, fire clay to line furnaces and millstone grit to provide silica for refractory bricks and the lining of later furnaces, meant that all the ingredients needed for iron making were readily to hand.

ABOVE: Blaenafon Works, 1922
RIGHT: Big Pit c.1910

In 1787 three businessmen from the English Midlands – Thomas Hill, Thomas Hopkins and Benjamin Pratt – leased the land on which Blaenafon now stands from the landowner, Lord Abergavenny. Three furnaces were constructed and in 1789 the first iron was produced. Blaenafon ironworks were the first multi-furnace works in Wales, and by 1796 had become the second largest in the country. These ironworks created the first large scale demand for coal in the area, and many mines were opened to meet the demand: more than 162 drift mines and 34 shafts have been recorded in the Blaenafon area.

Although Big Pit (then known as Kearsley's Pit) was first sunk prior to 1860, it is actually an amalgamation of several separate mines and has a very complex history. Mining started on the site with Forge Level (c.1812), followed by the Forge (c.1835) and the Coity Pits (c.1840), all of which supplied coal and ironstone to the Blaenafon Ironworks. Kearsley's Pit seems to have been used as a ventilation shaft, although it may also have wound coal or ironstone before 1880. In 1880 Kearsley's Pit was renamed Big Pit after having its diameter and depth increased.

At this time Big Pit became both the downcast and main coal winding shaft for Forge Level, Forge Pit and the Coity Pits. The Coity Pits were later sealed and fitted with an extractor fan and acted as the 'upcast' ventilation shaft for all the above pits as well as Dodd's Slope, a separate mine already connected to the Coity Pits. Later, yet another mine, Forge Slope, became part of the complex.

MINING AT BIG PIT

The rationalisation that created Big Pit seems to have been as a response to one of the periodic slumps in the iron industry, with the aim of increasing sale coal production, but it is likely that some ironstone was also mined in the early years. In 1896, 528 men were employed, producing gas, house and steam coal. By 1908, the manpower had risen to 1,145. In the same year, on 11 December, three men were killed at Big Pit in a localised explosion.

In 1947, Big Pit became part of the National Coal Board. Within a decade the whole of the mineral take for the Blaenafon and Abersychan areas was merged into one scheme centred on the colliery.

In 1967 Big Pit began working the Garw seam, using fully mechanized methods. The colliery was renamed Blaenafon New Mine in 1973 when a drift was driven to the surface from workings in the Garw seam, which had a maximum thickness of only 30 inches. This drift conveyed coal directly to the washery and the Big Pit shaft ceased winding coal and was used only for occasional man riding and the carriage of supplies. Around 500 men were employed at this time.

The last coal face stopped work in November 1979, and the colliery closed in February 1980 due to the exhaustion of workable reserves. At that time it was the oldest working coal mine in Wales.

ABOVE: Big Pit, 1975
OPPOSITE: Miners sitting by the air receiver, 1973

WHY 'BIG PIT'?

Big Pit was named after the width of its shaft, which is elliptical and 5.5 metres at its widest point, the biggest in the Blaenafon area at that time. Most local cages were designed to wind one dram at that time, but Big Pit's shape and size allowed two drams to be loaded into the cage side-by-side.

A FAMILY PIT

There was something special about working in Big Pit, partly because of its location on the edge of the coalfield.

It was a pit apart in every sense. There was a tremendous atmosphere here. It was more of a family pit than any other I'd ever known. The men would all intermix and help each other out, and the standard of workmanship was the highest possible.

The sense of comradeship would spill out into the men's leisure time. They'd go to rugby matches and concerts together. And the town would be bustling at a very early hour. If you walked through Blaenafon at a quarter to six in the morning, the shops would be open and there'd be up to a dozen buses crammed full of miners.

There were great characters working in Big Pit and the men were very fond of giving each other nicknames. One of them was known as Hot Feet because he was always rushing around. Another was Snow Shoes because he trudged through deep snow to get to work. A man from north Wales was known as Dickie North. And then there was Dry Bread – they called him that because of something he'd said.

'There was no malice in this – it was all good fun. Mining is a serious business and it's not only physically tough but hard mentally as well, because of all the danger around you. A sense of humour is a tremendous asset. The relationship between the management and the men was very good. During the miners' strike early in the '70s there was no acrimony at all. In fact, I used to have a cup of tea with the pickets.

I had to finish here because of ill-health, three years before the pit closed. I was sorry to leave the job and came away with many happy memories. I'd never been in a pit like it in all my life.

Aubrey Flynn, Big Pit under-manager, 1970s

THE COAL OWNERS

Early coal mines, like most of those in Blaenafon, were usually operated by the owners of iron or copper works. Most of the coal produced was used in their works, but they were always prepared to sell off any surplus. This part of the business increased as the sale coal industry flourished after the middle of the nine-teenth century, and the profits from the coal often helped the iron companies survive periodic slumps in the iron trade.

The individuals and partners who founded the steam coal companies after 1840 came from a variety of backgrounds. Some had started work in the metal and coal industries as engineers or mineral agents, such as W. T. Lewis who became Lord Merthyr and was one of the most powerful coal owners. David Davies of Llandinam had been a contractor who had gained fame as a railway builder in mid-Wales.

Other owners were merchants, ship owners or even shopkeepers. Individuals could set up the early collieries because little money was needed to begin mining operations. However, as mines became deeper and more expensive equipment was needed they had to take on partners or form limited liability companies.

Mining... is an industry which requires an extensive capital, highly technical knowledge, skill and considerable business capacity.

H. Stanley Jevons, The British Coal Trade *(1915)*

Who made the mine owner? Say the black bells of Rhondda

The Bells of Rhymn
Idris Dav

ABOVE: D. A. Thomas, *Cambrian Combine*
MIDDLE: W. T. Lewis, *Lewis Merthyr Collieries*
BELOW: Archibald Hood, *Glamorgan Collieries*

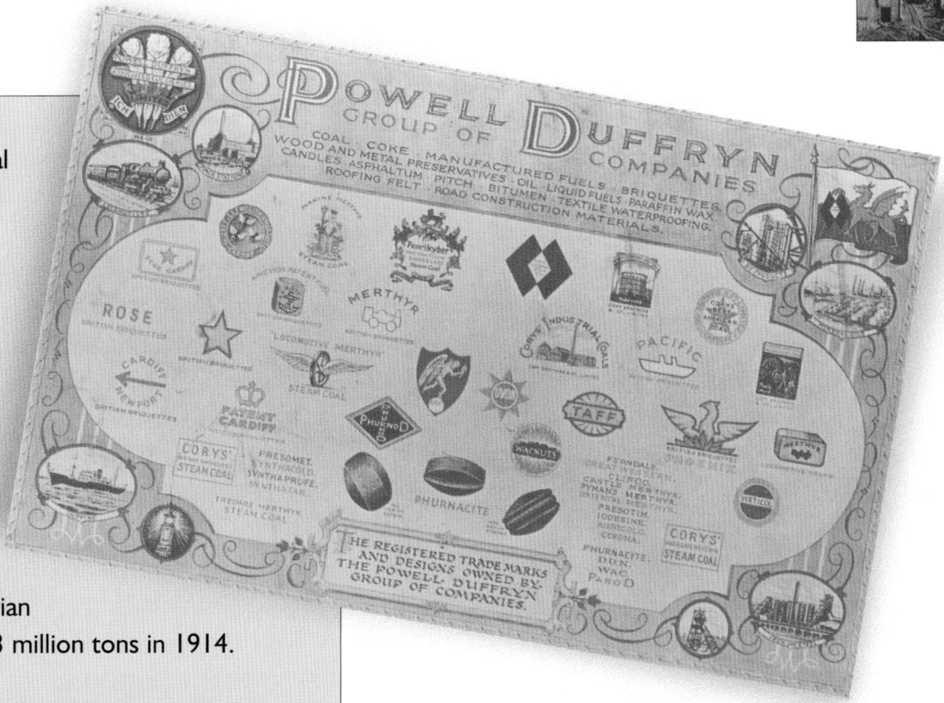

By the end of the nineteenth century most of the major coal companies had been formed. Many of them were the old iron companies, including the Blaenavon Iron and Steel Company Ltd, which by 1873 had become the second highest coal producer in Wales. Many smaller companies were swallowed up by larger ones to form giant 'coal combines', such as the Cambrian Combine, which produced 7.3 million tons in 1914.

The ironmasters had invariably been English, but the early coal owners were usually Welshmen. They lived locally and, like the majority of their workforce, spoke Welsh, were Nonconformist in religion and Liberal in politics. Many tried to improve the lot of their workers, opening schools, libraries, hospitals and chapels.

However, by the twentieth century most of the coal owners had moved out of the communities and began to distance themselves from their workforces. By the first decades of the twentieth century the miners were wary of the attitude of the giant coal combines towards them.

The miner now realises that he is considered merely as a cog in the great mining machine; he doesn't know his employer, he only knows of some limited company.

Noah Ablett, What we Want and Why *(1922)*

In 1947 the coal industry was nationalised and the coal owners passed into history, after receiving generous compensation: few tears were shed at their going.

WINNING THE COAL

Coal mining started around the rim of the south Wales coalfield where the seams came close to the surface and the coal could be dug straight from the ground. Known as 'outcropping' or 'patching', this method had the advantage of cheapness – underground mining needed greater amounts of money to be spent before the coal could be reached. Evidence of 'patching' is still visible to the north-east of Blaenafon town.

Later, 'drift' mines were driven into the hillsides to reach the coal, or less usually, 'bell pits' or shallow shafts were sunk. These were usually short lived and small scale, using simple technology. As the need for large scale mining increased to meet the demands of the industrial revolution, extraction methods became increasingly complex.

Until the later nineteenth century coal at Big Pit, as in the rest of Wales, was worked by the 'pillar and stall' system. In this system the stall was the area of coal hewed out and filled into drams by the collier and his assistant while pillars of solid coal were left to support the roof. This system was largely superceded by the 'longwall' system by which the coal was extracted from a long continuous coalface worked forward to remove all the coal in one operation.

Colliers 'undercutting' c.1910

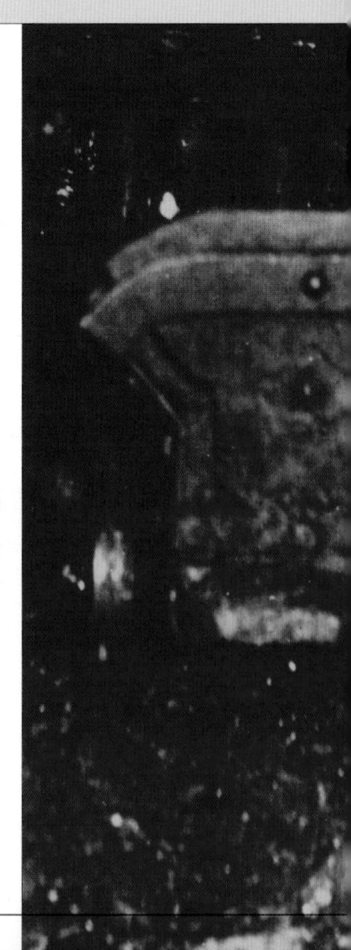

It took me weeks to learn the way of swinging elbows and twisting wrists without moving my shoulders. This holing under the coal was deadly monotonous work.

Bert Coombes, These Poor Hands *(1939)*

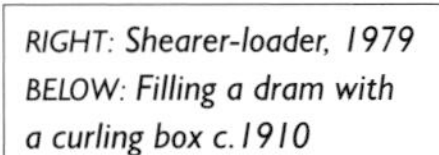

RIGHT: *Shearer-loader, 1979*
BELOW: *Filling a dram with a curling box c.1910*

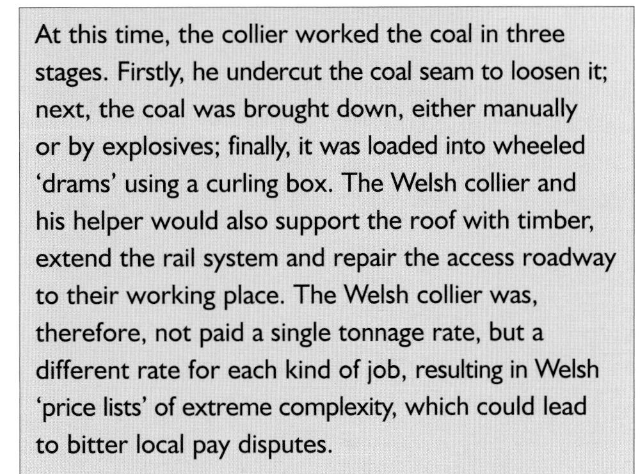

At this time, the collier worked the coal in three stages. Firstly, he undercut the coal seam to loosen it; next, the coal was brought down, either manually or by explosives; finally, it was loaded into wheeled 'drams' using a curling box. The Welsh collier and his helper would also support the roof with timber, extend the rail system and repair the access roadway to their working place. The Welsh collier was, therefore, not paid a single tonnage rate, but a different rate for each kind of job, resulting in Welsh 'price lists' of extreme complexity, which could lead to bitter local pay disputes.

Although practical coal cutting machinery had been available at the start of the twentieth century, coal cutting in Wales was mainly carried out by hand tools until after the nationalisation of the coal industry in 1947. There was then an intensive programme of coal face mechanization as machines which both cut and loaded the coal onto conveyors were introduced. One of these was the coal plough, introduced in Big Pit in the 1950s. This planed off a section of coal as it was pulled along the face by a chain. Also introduced at this time was the shearer-loader – a machine for cutting and loading coal by means of a rotating drum. By the mid-1970s, the latter type of machine was producing eighty per cent of all coal cut in Britain.

TRANSPORT

The early transport of coal and metals relied on pack animals. The building of canals such as the Monmouthshire and Glamorganshire canals and their linking tram roads greatly improved the situation in the late eighteenth and early nineteenth centuries. In north Wales, the river Dee played a similar role. However, the crucial factor in opening up the coalfields from the mid-nineteenth century was the development of a good railway system.

The Taff Vale Railway joined Merthyr Tydfil to Cardiff in 1841 and branch lines into the Rhondda and Cynon valleys opened soon after. By 1852 the TVR was linked to the Great Western Railway, which connected south Wales to the English Midlands and London, and branch lines gradually connected each of the mining valleys to the ports. The railways not only opened up the coalfield to the ports, but also made it easier for many miners to get to work.

With an effective railway system in place the Welsh coal ports expanded rapidly. The West Bute Dock at Cardiff was built in 1839 and heralded the rise of the docks at Barry, Penarth and Newport from 1850. Blaenafon shipped its coal through Newport, which was exporting 5,465,713 tons by 1914, but that figure was dwarfed by Cardiff, which exported 10,278,963 tons. The Barry docks were built by David Davies of Llandinam and other Rhondda coal owners to avoid the high charges of Cardiff docks. A new railway (the Barry Line) was laid from Rhondda, and in 1914 Barry exported 10,875,510 tons and so rivalled Cardiff for the title of the greatest coal exporting port in the world.

The situation at Blaenafon mirrored that elsewhere in south Wales. Initially the iron and coal was taken south, down the valley to Pontypool, first by pack animals and then by tram road. With the coming of the Brecon and Abergavenny canal a new tramway (Hill's Tram Road) was built to take the iron and coal east over Blorenge Mountain and through a tunnel more than a mile long down to the canal at Llanfoist.

The first railway line to reach Blaenafon from Pontypool was that of the Great Western Line in 1854. Iron and Coal from Blaenafon could now be transported direct to the wharfs at Newport.

The London and North Western Line reached Blaenafon in 1869 and continued northwards from Blaenafon High Level station to Waenafon and Brynmawr. The station at Waenafon was the highest in England and Wales.

Their land was laced with canals, roads, tramways, many of them triumphs of engineering

Gwyn Alf Williams, When Was Wales (1985)

DEATH, DISASTER AND RESCUE

THE TOLL

Because of the fiery nature of the deeper seams, Wales has been plagued by mining disasters. Between 1850 and 1920 one third of all British mining deaths were in Wales. There were twenty-seven major disasters (i.e. those involving ten or more deaths) in Britain between 1890 and 1920: thirteen of these were in Wales.

North Wales was largely free of major disasters; however, in 1934 an explosion at Gresford Colliery killed 266 men. After Albion in 1894 with 294 fatalities, and Senghenydd in 1913 with 439, Gresford was the third worst disaster in Welsh mining history.

My father always said that there was more fuss if a horse was killed underground than if a man was killed. Men came cheap – they had to buy horses.

William Hyatt, survivor of Senghenydd disaster, 1913

RIGHT: *Senghenydd, 1913*
LEFT: *Milfraen disaster, 1929*

South Wales will become a huge charnel house...

Mining Journal, 1846

Blaenafon also largely escaped the kind of major disasters that affected other mining communities. Because of the town's position on the edge of the south Wales coalfield the pits were shallower and had relatively little dangerous gas. In fact, Big Pit was so free of gas that, until 1913, miners worked underground with open lights.

The worst disaster in Blaenafon occurred in 1838 when the Cinder Pit was flooded and fifteen miners were drowned, including two girls and two boys aged 10 and 12 years old. In 1908, three men were killed in a firedamp explosion. In 1913, three colliery officials were suffocated at Big Pit when they went underground to prevent a fire spreading after all the workmen had been brought up to safety. In 1929, nine men were killed in an explosion at the nearby Milfraen Colliery. Although breaches of the safety regulations were found to have occurred, the jury at the inquest returned a verdict of *'death by misadventure and not otherwise'*.

There were other dangers. Falls of roof and transport accidents have killed more miners than the more publicised explosions. Miners suffered eye-strain from poor light, ruptures from heavy lifting and deafness from noisy tools. Minor cuts became easily infected, and crawling and kneeling caused inflammation of the joints. And worst of all, thousands died, and are still dying, a slow lingering death from lungs choked with mine dust.

Safety standards generally improved after the mines were taken into public ownership in 1947. High standards were achieved at Big Pit, which won three safety awards in 1977-8.

MINES RESCUE THE FOURTH EMERGENCY SERVICE

In spite of the increasing frequency of mining disasters during the nineteenth century, mines rescue was on an ad-hoc basis and relied on volunteers. In 1886 a Royal Commission recommended the establishment of rescue stations, but nothing was done until 1902 when a station was opened in Yorkshire, followed in 1908 by two stations in Wales at Crumlin and Aberaman. The opening of these early stations coincided with the development of practical breathing apparatus for use in rescue work.

At long last, in 1911 a Coal Mines Act compelled the owners to open rescue stations, and between 1911 and 1918 five more stations were opened in south Wales and two in north Wales. By the First World War, the terrible era of regular mining disasters was coming to an end, although major disasters did still occur well into the twentieth century.

After nationalisation of the coal industry in 1947, a national structure for mines rescue was developed. The rescue stations became a specialised, well trained and fully equipped force ready to deal with colliery fires, explosions and flooding, as well as civil disasters such as Aberfan in 1966. The last remaining station in Wales is located at Dinas in the Rhondda.

No soldier will face the bullets of an enemy more fearlessly than a collier will face death in the deadly afterdamp when the sacrifice of his own life may be the means of saving others.

Pontypridd Chronicle, 1 June 1901

Rescue team, Gresford colliery, 1939

Dinas Mines Rescue team at Merthyr Vale Colliery, 1980s

LIGHTING THE DARKNESS

Initially, mine lighting consisted of candles or simple open flame oil lamps, and such 'naked flame' lighting was still in use in shallower mine workings, including those at Big Pit, until the twentieth century. However, explosive gases and naked flame do not mix, and as mines became deeper mine lighting became a deadly problem.

Although the modern flame safety lamp is still known as a 'Davy lamp' it is actually an amalgamation of ideas. In 1812 Sir Humphrey Davy discovered that gauze placed around the flame of a lamp would prevent the ignition of gas outside that lamp. However, Davy's lamp was not ideal and it was modified by many other inventors to produce the modern flame safety lamp. Although it was gradually replaced as a source of mine lighting it continued to be used as a gas detector, as the flame changes shape and size when dangerous mine gases are present.

These lamps are difficult to use, for at the first shake the light goes out – probably when you need it badly. When the seam is warm or the air poor, the light will jump up in the glass, and that glass is blackened so that you have very little light. If the lamp slips just the least bit from the upright position, the flame dies out.

Bert Coombes, These Poor Hands *(1939)*

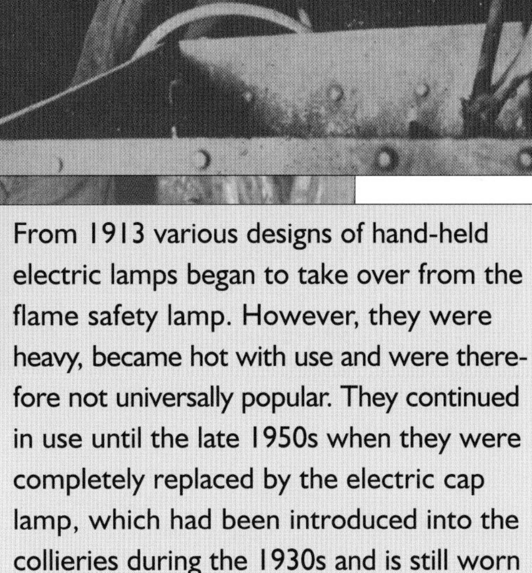

From 1913 various designs of hand-held electric lamps began to take over from the flame safety lamp. However, they were heavy, became hot with use and were therefore not universally popular. They continued in use until the late 1950s when they were completely replaced by the electric cap lamp, which had been introduced into the collieries during the 1930s and is still worn by visitors to Big Pit today.

In addition to the lamps carried by the miner, fixed lighting is provided at important areas underground such as pit bottoms and haulage houses. In the past this lighting had been provided by oil or compressed air lamps but mains-supplied tungsten lamps or fluorescent tubes are used today.

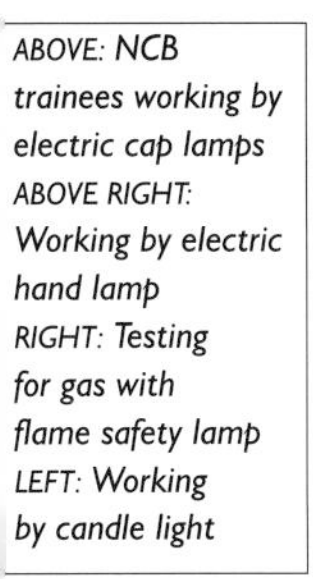

ABOVE: NCB trainees working by electric cap lamps
ABOVE RIGHT: Working by electric hand lamp
RIGHT: Testing for gas with flame safety lamp
LEFT: Working by candle light

WHAT DID MINERS WEAR?

White helmets and orange clothing are characteristic of today's mineworker, but this image is a fairly recent one. From early times until the mid-1970s miners had to provide their own working clothes, which usually followed the fashion of the day.

Clothes must be tough and not too tight; dirtiness is no bar, because they will soon be dirtier than they have ever been before. The usual wear is a cloth cap, old scarf, worn jacket and waistcoat, old stockings, flannel shirt, singlet and pants. Thick moleskin trousers must be worn to bear the strain of kneeling and dragging along the ground, and strong boots are needed because of the sharp stones in the roadways and the other stones that fall. Food must be protected by a tin box, for the rats are hungry and daring; also plenty of tea or water is necessary to replace the sweat that is lost.

Bert Coombes, *These Poor Hands* (1939)

RIGHT: 'The first day at work', Blaenafon, 1903
LEFT: Cartoon from Coal News, *1970s*

Fig. 100.—Woman and young miner of Pontypool.

By the 1970s miners were wearing flared jeans and tie-dyed t-shirts but were still carrying their food tins (or 'tommy boxes') and water jacks. The flat cap was replaced after the 1930s by a safety helmet, originally made of compressed cardboard, and by the late 1960s a plastic helmet similar to those worn at Big Pit today came into use.

The introduction of orange work clothes and a free laundry service in the 1970s put an end to the washing of filthy clothes at home. Three sets of clothing were provided – one to be worn, one in the wash and one for emergencies.

ABOVE: Pontypool coal miners, mid-nineteenth century
RIGHT: Orange work clothes, Tower Colliery, 1990s

COLLIERY HORSES

Colliery horses are often called 'pit ponies' by the general public, but in fact less than ten per cent of animals used in Wales were technically ponies.

The use of horses in mines increased during the late nineteenth century, especially after the 1842 Mines Act outlawed women and young children (who had previously provided most mine haulage) from working underground. By 1913, there were 70,000 colliery horses in Britain.

The south Wales coalfields employed some of the biggest horses in Britain. Welsh cobs standing at between 13 and 15 hands were preferred, but such was the demand that suitable horses were often imported from as far away as Russia and the USA. The coal-owners were generally believed to be more caring towards their horses than their men because of the greater expense involved. However, the men who worked with the horses would sometimes use harsh methods with a horse that they considered uncooperative or dangerous.

Of course, most horses were treated well and sometimes even spoilt by the miners who fed them with apples and sandwich crusts.

The last colliery horses in Britain were probably Robbie and Gremlin, who retired from a small mine at Pant y Gasseg, Pontypool in 1999.

Haulier and pony returning to the stables after working in Kear's Slope, 1965

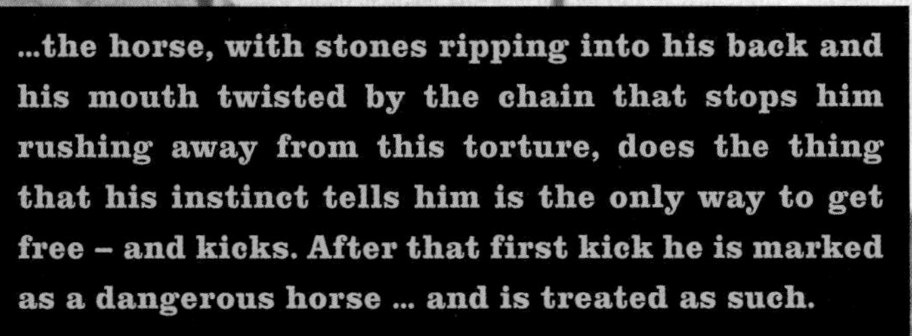

...the horse, with stones ripping into his back and his mouth twisted by the chain that stops him rushing away from this torture, does the thing that his instinct tells him is the only way to get free – and kicks. After that first kick he is marked as a dangerous horse ... and is treated as such.

Bert Coombes, These Poor Hands *(1939)*

Horse and haulier underground at Lewis Merthyr Colliery c. 1900

Miners riding colliery horses, National Colliery c.1910

WOMEN AND CHILDREN IN MINES

Until the mid-nineteenth century, it was normal for women and children to work in British coal mines. In Merthyr Tydfil in the 1840s, over fifteen per cent of the underground work started work at a very early age than in any other British colliery district.

Most children aged between five and eleven years old became 'door boys and girls' (or 'trappers') who opened and closed ventilation doors underground to allow men and coal to pass through. These children worked up to fourteen hours a day – often in complete darkness. Older children (usually fourteen to seventeen years old) often worked as 'trammers', moving the drams or sledges of coal to the main roadways that lead out of the mine.

The Children's Employment Commission was set up in 1840 to publicly expose the conditions under which children worked underground, although the commissioners were also shocked by the conditions of working women and described their hardships as well.

As expected, public opinion was outraged and a law was passed to stop child labour. Although it was now banned by law, many females and boys under the age of ten continued to work illegally underground until the 1860s, when Parliament made attendance at school compulsory. Women also continued to work legally on the surface as 'tip girls'. Even in the early twentieth century, children still started work as early as eleven years old and the school leaving age was not raised to fifteen until 1944.

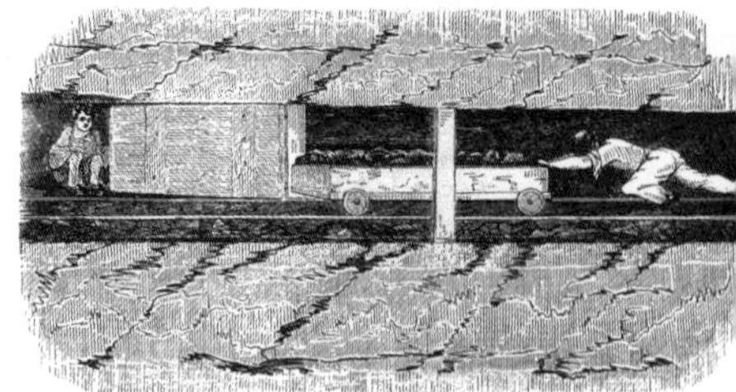

The work is very hard and I am running all day. My father is dead and my mother works in the colliery with my sister and three brothers. None of the boys in this pit wear shoes.

Benjamin Thomas, aged 8, Broadmoor Colliery, Pembrokeshire

Young miners in a training centre canteen c.1950

I have been below six or eight months and I don't like it much. I come here at six in the morning and leave at six at night. When my lamp goes out, or I am hungry, I run home.

Susan Reece, aged 6, Plymouth Mines, Merthyr Tydfil

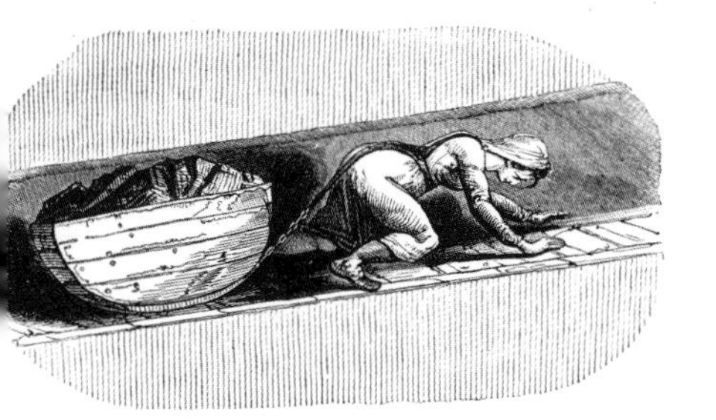

THE UNPAID SERVANTS OF THE MINES

Although the rapid expansion of the coal industry in the nineteenth century created a vast number of jobs for men, this was not the case for women.

In the Rhondda only fourteen per cent of females over the age of ten were recorded as being in paid employment. However, women in the mining communities were an important, albeit unpaid, part of the workforce.

Housework revolved around the shift pattern of the mine: in a large household miners were either coming in after one shift or preparing for the next. Pithead baths were not common until the 1930s, so one of the major tasks was boiling heavy tubs of water ready for the returning miner to take a bath; women also had to prepare meals, keep the house clean and look after children. They also had to juggle the finances carefully, as the piecework pay system meant that the amount of money coming into the household was never predictable and sometimes, especially at times of industrial unrest, non-existent.

One of the worst fears was that a husband or son would be brought home injured, or dead. However, being a collier's wife was a health hazard in itself. Pregnancy and child-birth, poor living conditions and heavy domestic labour were as dangerous to the women of the coalfield as the perils of the coal mine were to the miners.

After the 1940s, female employment became more common with the introduction of light manufacturing industries into the coalfields. This usually meant that a miner's wife worked her shift in the factory or office, and then went home to catch up with cleaning, cooking and childcare.

The women had to work harder than the men. After they'd come home, the men used to bath in front of the fire. Well you can imagine the mess that was on the kitchen after that, and the women then had to wash the kitchen floor.

Resolven woman, born 1902 (From Coal's Domain, 1993)

COLLIERY EXPLOSION—THE TWO WIDOWS, 1860 AND 1880

'THE FED'

The South Wales Miners Federation was formed in 1898 and by 1914 had become the largest single union in Britain with almost 200,000 members. In 1944 it became the National Union of Mineworkers, South Wales Area. It has always been regarded as one of the most militant trade unions, taking a leading role in UK-wide disputes from the Minimum Wage Strike of 1912 through the General Strike and Miners' Lock Out of 1926 to the last great strike of 1984-5.

The Fed also played a wider role in the life of the coalfield. Until after the Second World War, the mining villages were virtually single industry communities. Within the coal industry, this union dominated, and saw its role as a defender of these communities. As such, The Fed was involved with the domestic and social life of the people as well as under-taking the usual trade union activities. The Fed also had a wider influence in British trade unionism: three general secretaries of the Miners' Federation of Great Britain – Arthur Cook, Arthur Horner and Will Paynter – all came from within its ranks.

Two of the Union's social functions after the Second World War were the Miners' Gala and the Miners' Eisteddfod. The latter was established in 1948 and was the only trade union-sponsored festival of its kind. The Gala began as an essentially political gathering in 1953, but expanded to become a family outing with brass and jazz bands, sporting contests and art and craft exhibitions.

'Blacklegs', 1929

The Fed ... was a great deal more than a trade union. It was both an industrial and a social institution ... It differed from the normal functions of trade unions because of its more intimate involvement in the domestic and social life of the people.

Will Paynter, 'The Fed', in Men of No Property *(1971)*

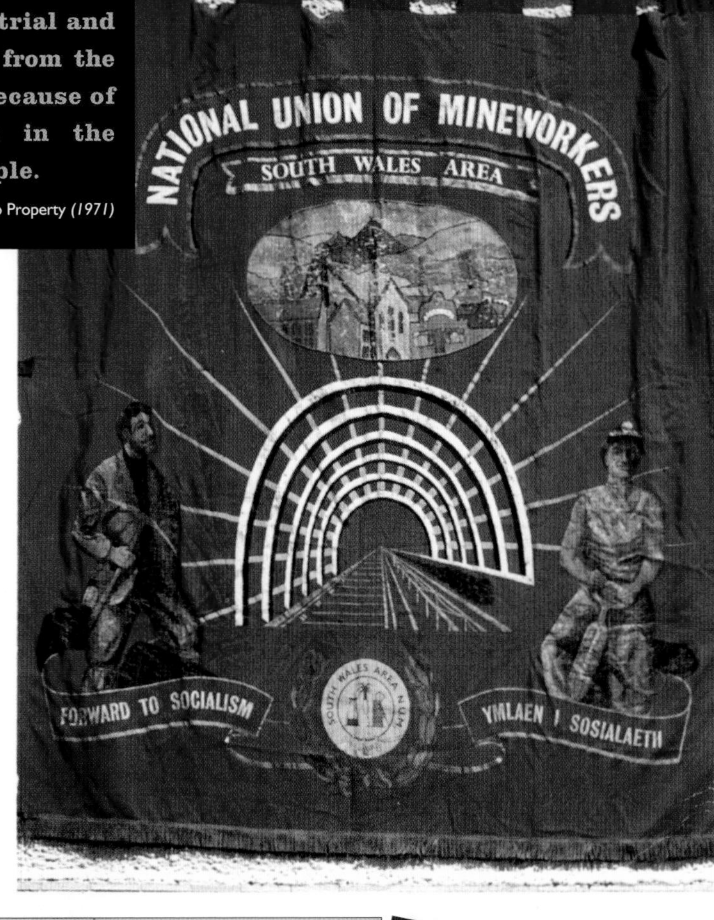

Pickets, 1984

The Miners' Call . . .
"Solidarity will win"

WELSH MINERS'
VICTORY
GALA DAY

★

PONTCANNA and SOPHIA GARDENS
SATURDAY, 10th JUNE, 1972

Souvenir Programme
10p

LEFT: NUM demonstration in support of steel strike, 1980

BEVIN BOYS

When war was declared against Germany in 1939, in spite of mining being a reserved occupation, thousands of experienced miners joined the armed services. Soon the government was desperate for men to take their places.

In December 1943, Ernest Bevin, the war-time Minister for Labour, devised a scheme whereby a proportion of conscripted men were sent into the collieries rather than the armed services.

Conscripts who refused to go into the mining industry were heavily fined or threatened with imprisonment. After being selected, the conscript was sent to one of the thirteen training collieries for a month's basic training before being sent to a colliery. He would either live in a purpose built hostel or lodgings.

Unlike the ordinary miners, 'Bevin Boys' as they became known were issued with overalls, safety helmet and working boots. The majority were employed as haulage workers rather than on the coal face.
A very small number stayed in mining after the war, but most couldn't wait to leave.

The last Bevin Boys were demobbed in 1948 but, unlike other conscripts, they received no service medals. It was not until 1995 that the UK government finally recognized their service to the war effort, and former Bevin Boys are now officially allowed to take part in the Remembrance Day service at Whitehall.

Bevin Boys and their instructors at Oakdale Colliery, 1944

It was once common for a son to follow his father and perhaps even his grandfather into the same mine and Big Pit is no exception. One of the many such families to have worked at Big Pit is the Grattons.

The dynasty started with Frank Gratton, who started working at Big Pit in 1904 and survived the fire of 1908 in which three men and a dog were killed when they and Frank descended the mine to save the horses. Frank himself was rendered unconscious by the fumes from the fire and was only saved when another group of rescuers found him. He became an official in 1910 and the colliery under-manager in 1914, a position he retained until he retired in 1956 after fifty-three years working underground.

Frank's son Graham started at Big Pit as an apprentice electrician shortly before his father retired, and went on to become a colliery electrical engineer at several mines before returning to Big Pit.

Keeping the family tradition going, Graham's daughter Heather began working in the shop in 2003.

Graham and Heather Gratton 2004

A former workman remembers Frank:

Frank Gratton was the under-manager then. He knew the pit inside and out and he was very well respected. He didn't like swearing and I remember once he came across a few of us when the language was a bit ripe. He ordered us to make a donation to Blaenafon Hospital to teach us a lesson – and we did too!

Big Pit rescue team, 1913. Frank Gratton is in the middle of the front row

SOME FACTS AND FIGURES

- The south Wales coalfield covers approximately 1,000 square miles
- There were 951 people in the Rhondda Valleys in 1851; by 1924, owing to the growth of the coal industry, there were 167,000
- More than 3000,000,000 tons of coal have been extracted from the Welsh coalfields
- There have been well over 1,500 coal mines in Wales
- 1913 was the peak year of production, with 56,830,317 ton extracted from south Wales alone
- In 1920 there were 271,000 miners in Wales
- In the 1930s Powell Duffryn of south Wales became the largest colliery company in Europe
- By 1935 the number of miners in south Wales had dropped to 130,000
- Between 1957 and 1964 50 collieries closed in south Wales
- Between 1851 and 1920 there were 48 major mining disasters in south Wales
- Between 1890 and 1920 a third of all UK mining related deaths occurred in Wales
- The worst mining disaster in Britain occurred at Senghenydd Colliery in 1913, with 439 deaths
- By 1914 the South Wales Miners Federation was the single largest trade union in Britain with almost 200,000 members
- Three general secretaries of the British miners' union came from Wales – Arthur Cook, Arthur Horner and Will Paynter
- The South Wales Miners' Eisteddfod was the only festival of its kind to be sponsored by a trade union
- Only 6% of the 20,000 south Wales miners broke the strike in 1984-5
- In 1984 there were 30 major Welsh collieries; by 2004 only one deep mine remained

Glossary of mining terms

BANKSMAN
The person in charge of the shaft at the surface of a colliery.

CURLING BOX
A three-sided steel scoop with handles on each side, used to carry lump coal from the coal face to the dram.

DRAM (OR TRAM)
The common Welsh term for a small truck used to carry coal or supplies.

DRIFT
A mine entrance or road inclined from the surface.

FIREDAMP
An explosive gas consisting mainly of methane.

FIREMAN
The Welsh term for a safety official underground.

HAULIER
A man who worked with horse-drawn transport underground.

MANDREL
The Welsh term for a miner's pick.

ROADWAY
Any mine passage or tunnel.

TIMBERMAN
A worker responsible for placing timber supports in the mine.

TOMMY BOX
A small metal container used to carry food underground.

A TOUR OF BIG PIT

A TOUR OF BIG PIT

Match the numbers with those on the map

1

RECEPTION AND SHOP

This building was originally associated with a completely separate mine called Dodd's Slope, which you can learn more about later in the tour. The building was once the compressor house for Big Pit, and later became the fitting shop.

In the early days most underground equipment was either made or repaired at the mine and two of the original machines, a lathe and a drill used for this purpose, are on display near the entrance.

The building has three sets of wide entrance doors to enable large pieces of equipment to be brought into the building.

Today the building is clean, neat and welcoming, a far cry from when it was filled with dirty, greasy machinery.

Fitters operating block and tackle

THE BOILER YARD

On leaving Reception, there is a large open space to the left where the steam boilers for the colliery once stood. The boilers in this area powered much of the surface machinery, including the winding engine which wound men, materials and coal through the shaft.

During the early twentieth century electrical power gradually replaced steam power in mines. At Big Pit the use of steam stopped around 1953, after which the boilers in this area were demolished.

From here you can see the sidings for railway wagons which, after loading with coal, joined the hundreds of trains that once flowed out of the mining valleys towards the coast. Blaenafon coal was usually taken to the docks at Newport, and from there it was sent all over the world.

Big Pit c.1901

Richard Hanbury begins exploiting the minerals and timber of Blaenafon for his ironworks at Pontypool

150 AD | **1248** | **1565**

The Romans smelt iron using local ore and coal at their fort at Caerleon

Earliest written reference to use of coal in Wales (Neath)

2

THE WAITING ROOMS

This building is now set aside for visitors waiting to take the

underground tour, but it once housed the electrical workshops and stores, where the maintenance and repair of the electrical equipment used at the mine was carried out. On the ceiling are the sturdy eye bolts that were once used to winch heavy equipment from drams on to the floor or workbenches.

Attached to the waiting rooms are the offices that were used by the colliery manager and his senior staff. The timekeeper's office has been restored and the officials' lodge has been converted into a first aid room, but most of the offices are still being used for their original purposes.

Officials walking from the lodge, 1973

HOURS OF WORK

In 1842, when the first reliable figures became available, colliers worked up to twelve hours a day. This decreased to around ten hours by 1890. After the passing of the Eight Hour Act in 1908, colliers worked five 8-hour shifts between Monday and Friday and a 4-hour shift on Saturday.

In 1947 a 5-day week was introduced and by the 1960s miners were working 37 hours a week – around half that worked by their great grandfathers.

The officials' lodge

The first major shafts in Blaenafon, Old Coal Pits, are sunk

Forge level, later incoprorated into Big Pit, opens

1787 1792 1800 1812

Thomas Hill, Benjamin Pratt and Thomas Hopkins open Blaenafon Ironworks

Monmouthshire Canal started

4 THE UNDERGROUND TOUR

Big Pit's famous underground tour has changed little since the colliery was first opened to the public in 1983. After the visitor has been lowered 90 metres (300 feet) down the mineshaft, the tour consists of a 50-minute walk around a section of original underground workings including stables, engine houses and coal faces in the company of a former coal miner. During the tour the visitor wears the same equipment – helmet, cap lamp, belt, battery and 'self rescuer' – used by miners. The guides will explain the different ways in which coal was mined and transported, and sharesome of their own experiences.

Group of miners at the pit top, 1976

H. S. JEVONS in *The British Coal Trade* (1915) describes the collier's work as requiring *'...seven or eight hours of almost incessant strenuous physical exertion... working continuously, as some must do, in a dripping wet place generally leads to diminished vitality and disease. Whilst some seams are very wet, others are too dry, so that there is constantly coal dust in the air which is somewhat unwholesome to breathe and highly dangerous.'* On top of this the miner faced a walk of up to three miles to the shaft at the end of his shift, which, in wet mines, could mean a *'...trudge through pools of black slush, water percolating from the roof.'*

Gate Road in Garw Seam,

Cage full of men waiting to descend, 1973

5

PIT BANK, TRAM CIRCUIT AND LAMPROOM

Today the area around the top of the shaft, or the 'pit bank' as it is usually known, can be a very busy place with visitors setting off for and returning from their underground tours.

The pit bank was always a noisy, busy place, with men and materials descending the mine and drams of coal emerging after their long journey from the coal face.

Tippler c.1975

The tram circuit

This is the route taken by the filled drams. Raised to the surface by cage, they ran along the rails by gravity to the 'tippler' or 'tumbler'. The tippler turned the tram upside down, emptying the coal on to screening belts where it was graded into various sizes according to market requirements. After the drams were emptied, they were hauled to a higher level by a heavy, motor-driven chain known as a 'creeper'. From here they were diverted out onto the stockyard to be filled with pit props before running back by gravity to the pithead, so completing the circuit.

Exterior view of the tram circuit c. 1975

The lamp room

The modern lamp room is a recent construction built on the foundations of the original building, which burnt down in the 1960s. The present building is a working area, used to maintain and charge the electric cap lamps used by both visitors and staff.

The lamp room, 1975

In a production colliery, the miner would enter the lamp room at the beginning of his shift to hand in his lamp check and pick up his electric cap lamp. At the end of the shift he would return his lamp to the charging rack to be recharged for the next shift, and the lamp man would give him his lamp check back. The checks were kept in the lamp room and could be used to determine who was underground at any one time; this was crucial in an emergency.

The Big Pit lamp man and his staff also look after that most easily recognised symbol of the coal industry – the flame safety lamp. Although only carried today by colliery officials as gas detectors, these lamps were once the miner's only source of light.

For more information about lighting underground, see *Lighting the darkness* on page 26.

1860	1875	1878	1880
Kearsley's Pit opens.	Sliding scale set up to decide miners' wages.	Bessemer Process for steel making discovered at Blaenafon.	Kearsley's Pit deepened, widened and renamed Big Pit.

6

THE STOCKYARD, SAWMILL AND MORTAR MILL

The stockyard

The stockyard is where the timber and other materials needed to work the mine were stored. When coal was mined by hand, large quantities of timber were needed to support the roof of the coalface and underground roadways. Every day timber brought in by train would be off-loaded here ready for use underground.

'Pit props', 1920s...

The sawmill

Some of the larger timbers would need to be cut down to size in the sawmill, which is still used for the same purpose today.

Young boys often started their mining careers in the sawmill before moving on to underground work. However, the surface of a mine can sometimes be as dangerous as the coal face:

... and 2004

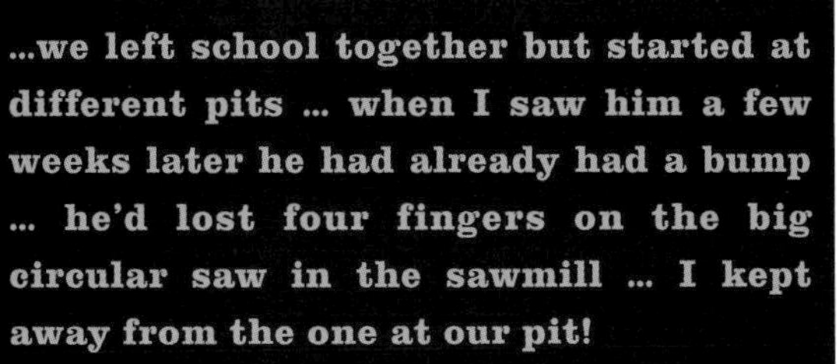

...we left school together but started at different pits ... when I saw him a few weeks later he had already had a bump ... he'd lost four fingers on the big circular saw in the sawmill ... I kept away from the one at our pit!

Peter Walker, Maerdy Colliery

The mortar mill

This is housed in the same building as the sawmill and was used to mix the mortar for building work on the surface and underground. The mill was used until the 1950s, but it was buried and forgotten until being rediscovered during building work in 2002.

THE WINDING ENGINE HOUSE

The winding engine is at the heart of our operation. The 'winder', as it is known, raises and lowers the cages carrying coal, men and materials up and down the shaft.

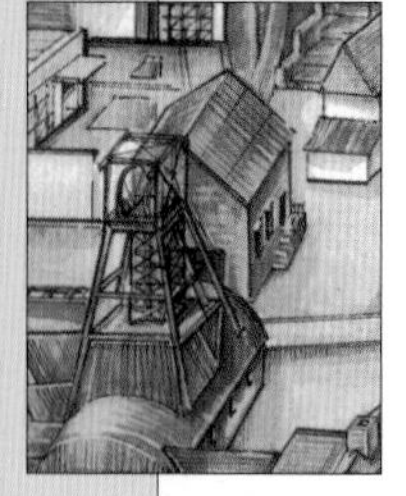

Big Pit's winding engine is no antiquated museum piece: even though the engine itself is over fifty years old, it is fully up to date with modern requirements and there are many safety systems and several computers controlling and monitoring its operation.

The winding engine man is always willing to discuss his work and the machine he operates. However, despite all the systems he has to help him, the job of the winding engineman remains a very responsible one and demands concentration – so please do not take flash photographs or do anything that might distract him while he's driving.

The driver's cab, 1975

The cable reels, 1975

The present winding house was built in 1952 as part of the improvements to Big Pit following the nationalisation of the coal industry in 1947. The previous steam-driven winder was replaced by the present electric version, which was built and installed by Uskside Engine Company of Newport.

The stone foundations and cast iron supports associated with the original nineteenth-century winding house are still visible outside the present structure.

Approximately twenty-five minutes at the beginning of each shift was allocated for the winding of the men. In Big Pit's heyday up to 400 men worked underground both on the day and afternoon shift and around 200 on the night shift. On a full shift, about 500 drams of coal would be raised.

The winding engine, 1975

ELLED'S SLOPE WINDING HOUSE AND PITMEN'S CABIN

Adjacent to the waiting rooms (see number 2) is a small red-roofed building which previously served as a winding house and pitmen's cabin.

The Elled winding house, centre, c.1970

Elled's Slope winding house

Most of this small building is known as the Elled Winder. This once housed the haulage engine or winch for Elled's Slope, which was a small drift mine opened in the late 1940s. This mine was abandoned in 1951 due to unsuitable geological conditions.

Although the entrance to the mine itself was sealed and is now buried under the car park, the haulage engine continued to be used to pull materials up to the tip for many years. Later the engine was removed and the building converted to use as a store, but we hope that we will soon be able to re-install an engine and put the building on display.

The pitmen's cabin

Behind the Elled winding house is the pitmen's cabin. In some coalfields the term 'pitman' is another name for a mineworker; in Wales, they are the men who maintain the mine shaft. Because they work in such dangerous and difficult conditions, they wear safety harnesses and use other specialised equipment. Some of this equipment can be seen inside the cabin.

At the corner of this building you can see the damage caused over the years by drams of equipment being taken to the electrical workshop for repair.

THE BLACKSMITHS' YARD

The group of buildings around this yard are some of the oldest buildings on site and date from the 1870s.

The left-hand wing is the fitting and welding shop, which is still in use today.

The central part of the group was the blacksmiths' shop. There were originally nine working forges in the building, of which four remain. Two of these are still used regularly by Big Pit's blacksmith.

In a working colliery the blacksmiths made and repaired anything and everything – drams, rail junctions, pipes, spanners and hammers. If you gave them a sketch of an object, they could make it.

Big Pit blacksmiths, 1952

The blacksmiths were also responsible for making horse shoes. Patterns were taken for each individual horse to replace worn or damaged shoes. The shoes were made on the surface and then taken underground where the horse would be shod.

The horses used on the surface of the mine were stabled alongside the forges. Originally their stables occupied the entire wing of the building. The stables for the horses that worked below ground can be seen on the underground tour.

The blacksmith at work today

Part of the surface stables was converted into an electrical workshop in the 1950s. This is now an education room.

The blacksmiths' shop and yard, 1974

1913 Peak year for south Wales coal output – 56,830,072 tons from over 600 collieries.

1913 Three men killed in an underground fire at Big Pit.

1913 Flame safety lamps introduced at Big Pit.

1916 Coal industry taken over by government.

THE CAFÉ

This building was erected during Big Pit's life as a museum

on the site of several timber buildings that had been in use when the mine was in production. Panels around the walls show the influence of Italian cafés on the life of the mining communities.

8

THE MINING GALLERIES

The mining galleries are simulated underground workings set into the hillside above the colliery. They house a multi-media presentation telling the

story of how the Welsh mining industry evolved from that of the collier craftsmen into the sophisticated, mechanised modern industry of today.

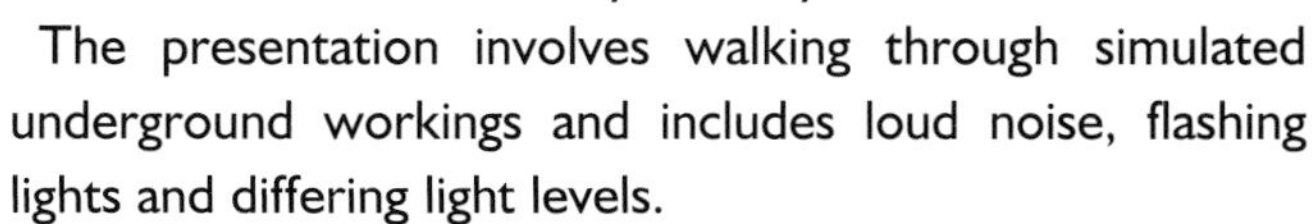

The presentation involves walking through simulated underground workings and includes loud noise, flashing lights and differing light levels.

1921 — *Peak manpower in south Wales coalfield – 271,000.*

1921 — *Coal industry handed back to coal owners, followed by miners defeat in lock out, wages reduced.*

1926 — *General strike and lockout, miners defeated, longer hours and reduced wages.*

9 THE FAN HOUSE

This is one of the most important buildings at any coal mine. The ventilation system brings oxygen into the mine, removes or dilutes unwanted gases, dust and fumes and provides a cooler and dryer environment for the miners to work in.

The original ventilation system at Big Pit relied on furnaces near the bottom of the Coity shafts, and the concrete covers of these can be seen at the northern end of the building. The furnaces warmed the stale air, which then rose up these shafts, to be replaced by fresh air drawn down the shaft that visitors now descend.

The original fan house was built in 1896 to accommodate the steam-powered Waddle fan that replaced the furnaces.

That fan house was replaced by the present building, which was built in 1910 to accommodate the electrically powered Walker fan that can be seen today.

Even though the fan attendant only had to check the fan every two hours, the fan house had to be manned twenty-four hours a day, so in most mines the fan attendant was given other jobs to do as well.

As a result, Big Pit's fan house was extended over the years to accommodate a telephone exchange for the mine and the compressors used to generate the compressed air needed to power tools and equipment underground.

The telephone exchange c.1976

The fan house c.1936 (the Pithead Baths are not yet built)

4

THE EXPLOSIVES MAGAZINE

The explosives or 'powder' magazine at every mine was always built away from other buildings in case of an accidental ignition of its contents. The building was also designed so that any internal explosion would blow up through the roof or the back wall, away from the main parts of the site.

The shotsman inserting explosive charge in a shot hole

The explosives and detonators used to break up stone and coal underground were stored here. The explosives were either sent underground in special explosives drams or carried by workmen in explosives canisters – but only the shotsman could handle the detonators.

The shotsman was a mine official trained in the use of explosives. He was responsible for charging up the shot holes drilled by the workmen, testing for gas and generally ensuring that the explosives were used safely.

The powder magazine, 1979

THE WATER BALANCE

The water balance as a winding engine at Brynpwllog Colliery, 1934

The water balance that has been re-erected near the powder magazine was the winding engine of Brynpwllog Colliery (or 'Rogers Pit') in the Rhymney Valley and dates from the mid-nineteenth century. It spent many years on display outside the National Museum & Gallery in Cardiff before being relocated to Big Pit.

This method of winding was very common in Wales during the first half of the nineteenth century and was used at several mines in Blaenafon, including Big Pit.

The water balance at Big Pit today

1944 South Wales Miners Federation becomes the NUM South Wales Area.

1947 Coal mines nationalised.

1965 Last major Welsh colliery explosion – 31 killed at Cambrian Colliery.

10 PITHEAD BATHS

Walking through the pithead baths today, it is difficult to imagine the great impact such buildings had on the lives of the miner and his family. Prior to the introduction of baths, the miners had no option but to travel home dirty and wash in a tin bath in front of the fire or outside in the 'bailey' (back yard).

The gradual introduction of baths during the first half of the twentieth century was part of a wider movement of social reforms aimed at creating a more just society, which included the introduction of old age pensions, votes for women, the national health service and the nationalisation of most of Britain's strategic industries.

The pithead baths at Big Pit was opened in 1939 and was built in the continental International modernist style favoured by the architects of the Miners' Welfare Committee, which was the body responsible for all such buildings.

The 'dirty' lockers, 1976

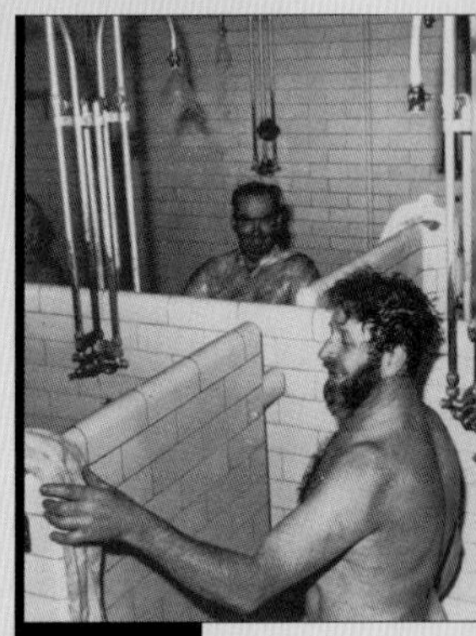

Men bathing

HOW THE BATHS WORKED

Each miner was provided with two lockers located in different parts of the building. The miner would leave his ordinary clothes in his 'clean' locker before walking across to his 'dirty' locker carrying his tommy box (food container), towel and soap dish. Here he would put on his working clothes, fill his water bottle, grease his boots (on Tuesdays and Thursdays only) and make his way to the top of the pit for his shift underground.

After his shift, the miner undressed and left his work clothes in his dirty locker where they would be dried ready for his next shift by hot air constantly blowing through the lockers.

The pithead baths boiler house, 1979

1966 — Aberfan tip slide kills 144 people, including 116 schoolchildren.

1967 — *The first fully mechanized coal face is installed at Big Pit.*

1972 — *First national miners' strike since 1926.*

1972 — *Horses cease working underground at Big Pit.*

How the baths worked (cont)

After bathing he dressed and made his way home, perhaps stopping on the way for a cigarette and a cup of tea in the canteen.

Each miner had to provide his own towel and soap and usually kept a tin of Vaseline in his locker to clean the coal dust from his eyelids after bathing.

The Pithead Baths building houses four exhibition spaces, using objects and images to tell the story of coal mining in Wales.

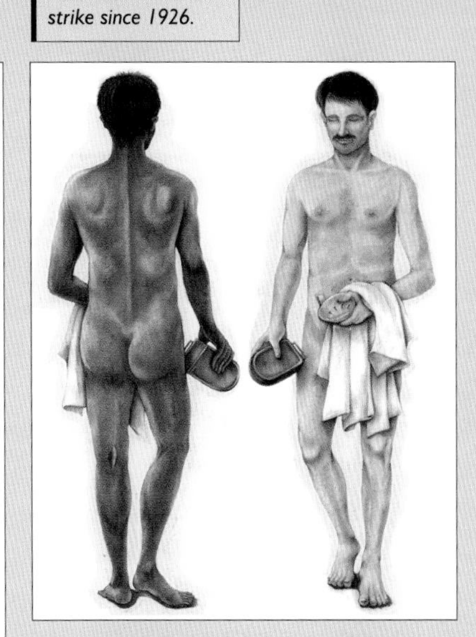

THE EXHIBITIONS

Exhibition Area 1

The Mineworker from 1850 to 2000

Exhibition Area 2

Children in the mines, health, home life and the mining communities.

> **Huge washing machines in which dirty miners went in at one end and clean ones came out at the other!**
>
> *Bert Coombes,* These Poor Hands *(1939)*

Exhibition Area 3

Geology, Surveying, Uses of Coal, The Colliery, Mine Lighting, Mines Rescue, Disasters, The Trades Unions, Nationalisation and Mining Memorabilia.

Exhibition Area 4

This is a multifunction space which serves as an education room, packed lunch room and lecture theatre. It also houses both temporary and permanent exhibitions.

The permanent exhibition deals with the controversial subject of energy sustainability.

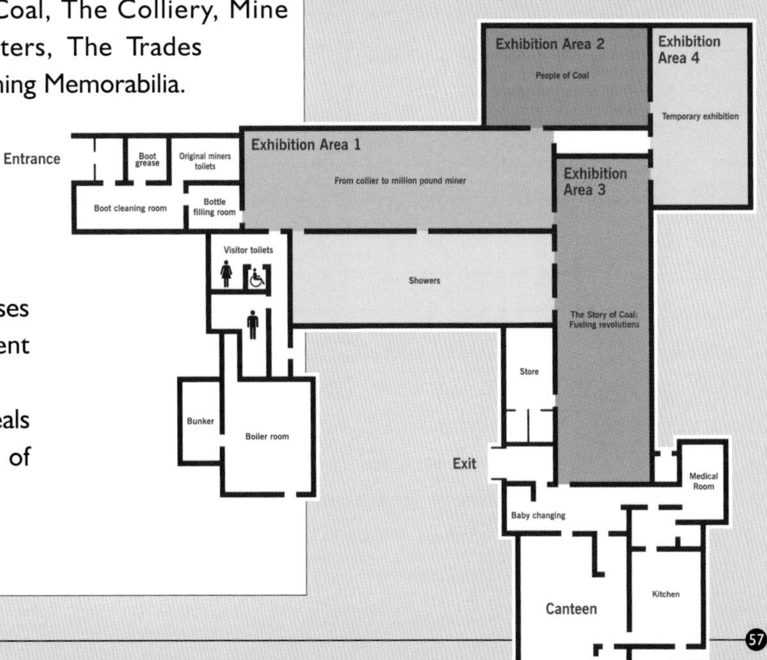

1973 — A new drift is sunk and Big Pit renamed Blaenafon New Mine.

1974 — National miners' strike.

1980 — Big Pit closes as a production mine.

11

THE CANTEEN

In addition to food, the canteen provided such items as chewing tobacco, snuff, soap, flannels, towels, tommy boxes (food tins), water bottles, baths slippers and even babies nappies! At the beginning and end of the shift it provided those most essential of items: a fag and a cup of tea.

The canteen in the 1970s

The canteen was sometimes used to hold pit head meetings if a dispute with the management arose. At times like these the canteen would be full of great speeches and bitter argument before the workforce decided whether to go to work or return home on strike.

There are no nappies or cigarettes on sale today, and the canteen is now an atmospheric licensed restaurant conveniently placed to provide hot meals and refreshments.

THE MEDICAL CENTRE

Big Pit's medical centre is near the canteen. After nationalisation in 1947, health and safety procedures improved, proper medical centres were built and medical centre attendants appointed.

Phyllis Jones, colliery nurse, Great Mountain Colliery 1957

In most collieries the medical centre attendants were men, but some nursing sisters were also employed and sometimes supervised the work of male colleagues.

Happily most of their hours were spent treating the day-to-day cuts, bruises and strains that miners had suffered. However, at times the attendants had to care for miners who had been seriously injured underground. The voice that you can hear in the medical centre is that of Mrs Phyllis Jones, a former colliery nurse in Cynheidre Colliery.

Big Pit opens as a museum.

1983 **1984-5** **1994**

National miners' strike.

Last British Coal mine in Wales, Tower Colliery, is closed; later reopens as workers' cooperative.

> *To them* [the miners] *the ambulance man represented the first face that they would see after their injuries had been sustained, a face that offered some promise of medical help – some hope that this person, the ambulance man, would preserve their life, prevent further damage and promote their recovery. Sadly, all too often, however, in this most arduous industry, the ambulance man's face was the last thing that they saw in this world.*
>
> *Arthur Parfitt b.1902, Ambulance man, Cwm Cynon Colliery*

The view c.1907...

... in 1951...

3

THE VIEW POINT

Blaenafon's important place in the development of today's industrialised world, and the remnants of this industrial past, led to the designation of the area as a World Heritage Site.

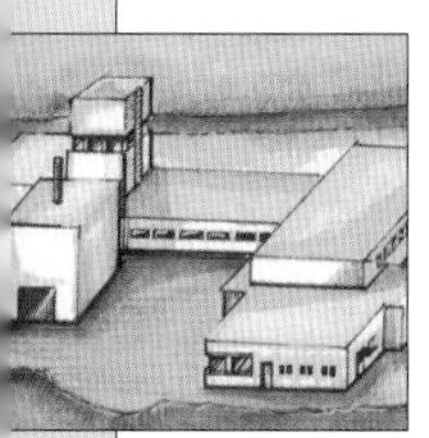

From the view point you can see many of these features, including Blaenafon Ironworks and its associated workers' housing, St Peters Church, numerous spoil heaps and tramroads and what remains of the former steelworks.

... and in 1975

THE STEPS

Because the only ground suitable to build the pithead baths was on the hillside above the main colliery site, flights of steps were built to connect the two areas.

If you find the climb daunting today, imagine how the colliers felt having to face these steps after a shift on the coalface!

On your left, at the bottom of the steps, are the fire station and the carpenters' workshop, both still used for their original purpose.

Miners climbing the steps to the pithead baths

December, Big Pit and much of the landscape around Blaenafon designated as a UNESCO World Heritage Site.

February, Big Pit is integrated into the National Museums & Galleries of Wales as Big Pit: National Mining Museum of Wales.

19

OPERATIONS AND RESOURCES BUILDING

This is the Museum's administrative centre, which also houses a small library with a collection of historical and technical books that researchers can use by appointment.

The site in 1969...

CONSERVATION WORKSHOP AND COLLECTIONS STORES

Big Pit holds the single most important collection of Welsh coal mining artefacts in existence, and it is in here that the National Coal Mining Collection of Wales is stored.

The Large Object Stores

The ground floor of the building houses examples of large mining machinery and is open to visitors at specified times.

The Small Object Stores

The upper floor houses the smaller objects in the collection and is open to the public by prior appointment or on special occasions.

The collection is fairly broad and covers the development of coal mining in Wales since the early eighteenth century. As well as the technological aspects, the collection also emphasise the more social and personal aspects of the coal mining industry.

There are around 5,000 objects in the collection, ranging from early wooden tools through to fan engines. One of the most important parts of the collection is the 1,500 items of mine lighting, from candle holders to armoured fluorescent tubes. Other parts of the collection cover hand and power tools, mine surveying, trade unions and disasters.

... and in 2004

Emergency mobile winding engine

Through the side windows of the large object stores you can see the Emergency Mobile Winder. This consists of two vehicles – a power unit, and a winch that is used to rescue people trapped underground if the ordinary winding arrangements fail. This is operated and maintained by the Mines Rescue Service and provides cover for all mines in south Wales and the west of England.

DODD'S SLOPE

Dodd's Slope is another drift mine that once operated from within the Big Pit site. Unlike Elled Drift, the engine house has now disappeared, but the mine entrance can still be seen to the left of the steps before you enter the shop.

Dodd's Slope was driven in around 1840 and worked the Three Quarter, Big and Elled coal seams. Ventilation of these workings was initially achieved by means of a 100-foot-deep furnace pit, which, until the 1960s, was visible behind the pithead baths. At a later date it was connected to the Coity Pits and Forge Slope for ventilation purposes.

Dodd's Slope closed on 5 May 1909 after sixty-nine years in production.

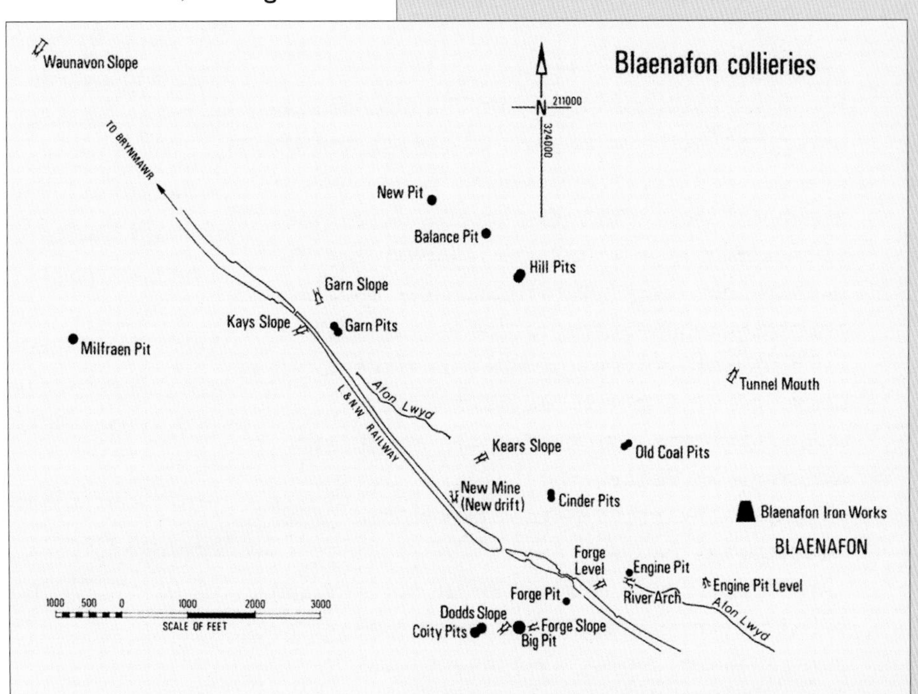

GENERAL INFORMATION FOR VISITORS

CONTACTING BIG PIT

Big Pit: National Coal Museum
Blaenafon, Torfaen, NP4 9XP
Tel: (01495) 790311 Fax: (01495) 792618
E-mail: bigpit@museumwales.ac.uk
Web: www.museumwales.ac.uk/bigpit

OPENING TIMES

Big Pit is open from 9.30 am to 5.00 pm daily. Please note the last underground tour is at 3.30 pm. Closed 25, 26 December and 1 January. Please telephone for opening times during December and January.

ACCESS

Big Pit is a coal mine on the side of a mountain, so physical access to some parts of the site can be difficult. An able-bodied helper is needed to accompany those with limited mobility. Some types of wheelchair may not be allowed on the underground tour but more suitable ones are available on request. Only four visitors in wheelchairs can be permitted underground at a time, in order to ensure safe evacuation in case of emergency.

Induction loops are installed at various points around the Big Pit site.

There are designated disabled parking bays on all three levels of the site.

An Access Guide is available on our website (www.museumwales.ac.uk/bigpit), at reception or by post on request.

THE SHOP

The shop sells gifts, souvenirs and general and specialised guides to the history of Wales and the coal industry. Other books we have published that might be of interest are:

Teyrnas y Glo / Coal's Domain
by Bill Jones and Beth Thomas (1993)

Big Pit, Blaenafon
by W. Gerwyn Thomas (1998)

For Those in Peril: civil decorations & lifesaving awards
by Edward Besly (2004)

In Search of Fossil Plants: The Life & Work of David Davies
by Barry A. Thomas (1986)

Welsh Coal Mines
by W. Gerwyn Thomas (1976, reprinted 1977, 1979, 1986, 1990)

Rhyd-y-car: a Welsh mining community
by Eurwyn Wiliam (2003)

Many fine authors and poets have worked in Welsh collieries:

Bert Coombes (1894-1974) worked as a collier in Resolven. His autobiography *These Poor Hands* (1939) was followed by two further books, *Those Clouded Hills* (1944) and *Miners Day* (1945). Anyone interested in learning about the mining industry should start here.

Idris Davies (1905-1953) was a poet who wrote from his experiences as a miner in the Rhymney valley. His published works are *Gwalia Deserta* (1938), *The Angry Summer* (1943), *Tonypandy and other Poems* (1945), *A Carol for the Coalfield* (2002) and *Collected Poems* (1953, reprinted 2003).

Lewis Jones (1897-1939) was a trade union activist who wrote two novels, *Cwmardy* (1937) and *We Live* (1939), which are outstanding depictions of Welsh mining life in the early twentieth century.

EATING AND DRINKING

Big Pit has two catering outlets, one of which is licensed. A range of menus is available for groups wishing to pre-book meals or buffets. Please telephone for further details.

FUNCTIONS

There are a number of rooms at Big Pit that are available for hire for functions or meetings. These rooms are only available at certain times of the year so please telephone for further details.

EVENTS

In addition to Big Pit's permanent exhibitions, a range of temporary displays, events, activities and demonstrations takes place throughout the year. Information on the current programme is available in our events listings, on the website (www.museumwales.ac.uk/events) or telephone for further details.

FACILITIES FOR SCHOOL GROUPS

A booklet entitled *Planning Your Visit* gives details for group visits, including the information needed for risk assessment. The booklet is free, please telephone to receive a copy by post.

GENERAL INFORMATION FOR VISITORS CONT.

The Blaenafon World Heritage Site

The Blaenafon Industrial Landscape, including Big Pit, was designated a World Heritage Site by UNESCO in 2000. Its unique industrial heritage has been recognised as being of international importance because it is one of the prime areas in the world where the full social, economic and technological process of industrialisation through iron and coal production can be studied and understood.

The town and landscape of Blaenafon contain a large number of individual monuments of the Industrial Revolution. Many are already accessible to the public, and others will become more so in the future.

Pontypool & Blaenavon Railway
Tel: (01495) 792263
Open: Every weekend Easter-end of September plus Bank Holiday Mondays

Blaenavon Ironworks
Tel: (01495) 792615
Open: April-Oct, Mon-Sun. Telephone for opening times outside this period. (Admission charged)

Blaenafon Community Heritage & Cordell Museum
Tel: (01495) 790911. Telephone for opening times

Blaenafon Booktown
Many book shops stocking a wide range of titles covering a wealth of subjects.
Open all year. For further details pick up a leaflet.
Tel: (01495) 793039

Tourist Information Centres
Blaenafon Tel: (01495) 792615
Abergavenny Tel: (01873) 857588

Monmouth & Brecon Canal
A tranquil haven for walkers and cyclists. Take a barge from Goytre Wharf or enjoy a picnic at Pontymoile Basin. Tel: (01873) 881069

Pontypool & Blaenavon Railway

Blaenavon Ironworks

Monmouth & Brecon Canal